HOW DO I DEAL WITH ANXIETY AND FEAR?

JOHN RAGSDALE

SMITH
FREEMAN
Publishing

ABOUT THE AUTHOR

John Ragsdale is a husband to Kristin, a dad to Evan & Davis, a singer-songwriter, a passionate communicator, and pastor of The Hills Nashville. John feels called to encourage people to be all that God created them to be.

@johnrags 🐦📷 [twitter & instagram] • johnragsdale.org [website] thehillsnashville.com

CONTENTS

A MESSAGE TO READERS

Here in the twenty-first century, fear is big business. Whether we turn on the evening news or go to the neighborhood movie theater or listen to radio on the way to work, we are bombarded by messages that are intended to induce fear, anxiety, apprehension, and hopelessness. We are reminded, time and again, that the world is a dangerous, unpredictable place. And we're encouraged to seek protection from a wide range of earthly protectors. But the ultimate source of protection comes, not from worldly sources, but from our Father in heaven.

Today and every day, the sun rises upon a world filled with God's presence and His love. As believing Christians, we have so many reasons to be hopeful: The Father is in His heaven, His love is everlasting, and we, His children, are blessed beyond measure. Yet sometimes we find ourselves distracted by the fears, the frustrations, and the uncertainties of daily life. But even during our darkest days, God never leaves us for an instant. And even when our hopes are dimmed, God's light still shines brightly. As followers of God's Son, we are called to search for that light—and to keep searching for it as long as we live.

The ideas on these pages are intended to help you live courageously and faithfully as you put all your earthly fears in perspective. This text celebrates the hope that springs from the promises contained in God's Holy Word. These pages contain Bible verses, quotations, essays, tips, and journaling prompts, all of which can lift your spirits and guide your path.

How desperately our world needs courageous Christians who are willing to honor God with their prayers and their service. May you be such a Christian, and may you share your courage and your wisdom with a world that needs both.

SEVEN STEPS
TO HELP YOU OVERCOME
ANXIETY AND FEAR

Understand That Fear Is One of Society's Greatest Commodities: Modern media constantly bombards you with fear-provoking, attention-grabbing headlines designed to capture your thoughts and redirect your life. Your task is to combat fear with faith.

Be Aware That the Enemy Wants You to Cower in Fear: Satan deals in fear, anxiety, deception, and doubt. God is about love, light, truth, and faith. Satan wants to control your thoughts and emotions. Your task, simply put, is to place your faith in the Creator and reject the devil's deceit.

Immerse Yourself in God's Word: Never stop studying God's Word. Even if you've been studying the Bible for many years, you've still got lots to learn. Bible study should be a lifelong endeavor; make it your lifelong endeavor.

Trust God's Promises: The Lord has made many promises to you, and He intends to keep every one of them. His promises give you faith, hope, and courage. When you are afraid, His promises will comfort you.

Guard Your Thoughts and Your Heart: God wants you to guard your mind and your heart from the anxieties and distractions that might cause you to stray from His path. When you encounter situations that make you afraid, turn your thoughts and prayers to your Creator. He will never leave you.

Measure the Size of Your Fears Against the Size of Your God: Whatever your problems, God is bigger. Much bigger. You must never forget that fact.

Be Optimistic: God's Word promises that if you've given your heart to Jesus, your eternal future is secure. So even when times are tough, you can be joyful, hopeful, and optimistic. Faith is stronger than fear. So if you want to defeat your anxieties and fears, you'll need the right kind of attitude—the positive kind.

1

THE QUESTION

It seems like I'm constantly gripped by vague, unspoken anxieties and fears. Why?

THE ANSWER

Fear is one of society's greatest commodities. Modern media constantly bombards you with fear-provoking, attention-grabbing headlines designed to capture your thoughts and redirect your life.

So, it's no surprise that you'll experience occasional fears and doubts. You can overcome those fears when you know who your enemy is, when you know who your God is, and when you know who you are.

The Lord Jesus by His Holy Spirit is with me, and the knowledge of His presence dispels the darkness and allays any fears.

BILL BRIGHT

FEAR NOT

Fear not, for I am with you; be not dismayed, for I am your God. I will strengthen you, yes, I will help you, I will uphold you with My righteous right hand.

Isaiah 41:10 NKJV

From time to time, all of us experience difficult days when unexpected circumstances that test our mettle. When these situations occur, fear creeps in and threatens to overtake our minds and our hearts. But God does not want His children to be fearful. He knows all too well that fear is a form of emotional slavery fostered by mankind's ultimate enemy.

Satan wants you to be afraid; he is about the unknown; he thrives on darkness, uncertainty, and fear. The Lord, conversely, is about certainty, and courage, and hope, and truth. Our Creator leads us to the light—His light. God promises us that we can know the truth and the truth will, indeed, set us free.

The phrase "fear not" is mentioned many times in the Bible. God's Word teaches us that earthly fears are temporary, but God's love is not. When we focus on His love and His Son, we can step beyond the boundaries of our fears and, by doing so, live the lives—and receive the blessings—that He intends.

Do you feel overwhelmed by vague fears or specific anxieties? If so, turn your concerns and your prayers over to your heavenly Father. Trust Him totally. Trust Him today. Trust Him always. And when it comes to the inevitable concerns and challenges of this day, hand them over to the Lord completely and without reservation. He knows your needs and will meet those needs in His own way and in His own time if you let Him. Your challenge, of course, it to let Him.

MORE FROM GOD'S WORD

*Even though I walk through the darkest valley,
I will fear no evil, for you are with me;
your rod and your staff, they comfort me.*
PSALM 23:4 NIV

Be not afraid, only believe.
MARK 5:36 KJV

*Peace I leave with you; My peace I give to you;
not as the world gives do I give to you. Do not let
your heart be troubled, nor let it be fearful.*
JOHN 14:27 NASB

But He said to them, "It is I; do not be afraid."
JOHN 6:20 NKJV

*For the LORD is good; His mercy is everlasting,
and His truth endures to all generations.*
PSALM 100:5 NKJV

MORE THOUGHTS ABOUT FEAR

*It is good to remind ourselves that
the will of God comes from the heart of God
and that we need not be afraid.*

WARREN WIERSBE

*Facing our deepest fears means making peace
with our seen self and with our unseen self.*

SHEILA WALSH

*The presence of fear does not mean
you have no faith. Fear visits everyone.
But make your fear a visitor and not a resident.*

MAX LUCADO

*When we face our fears,
we can find our freedom.*

JOYCE MEYER

*His hand on me is a father's hand,
gently guiding and encouraging.
His hand lets me know he is with me,
so I am not afraid.*

MARY MORRISON SUGGS

REMEMBER THIS

If you're feeling fearful or anxious, you must trust God to solve the problems that are simply too big for you to solve on your own. With God as your partner, you have the power to face your fears and rise above them. Whenever you're paralyzed by fear, it's not that you don't have the power; it's that you don't know you have the power.

GET PRACTICAL

Are you feeling anxious or fearful? If so, trust God to handle those problems that are simply too big for you to solve. Entrust the future—your future—to God. The two of you, working together, can accomplish great things for His kingdom.

A CONVERSATION STARTER

Talk to a friend about the kinds of fears that may be holding you back.

NOTES TO YOURSELF

Write down your thoughts about the role that fear plays in your life. Are you too fearful? If so, in what ways are your fears holding you back?

Sometimes I let the fear consume me of what needs to happen and what will happen. When we cant pay bills or how will we make it or buy groceries

2

THE QUESTION

When times are tough, I feel anxious and afraid. I know that I need courage. Where can I find it?

THE ANSWER

When you are fearful, you must focus on God's power, not your own perceived weanesses.
Work as if everything depended on you
and pray as if everything depended on Him.
Fear has one goal: to control you.
But God has other plans, and He wants you
to trust Him in good times and hard times.

*Whatever clouds you face today, ask Jesus,
the light of the world, to help you look behind
the cloud to see His glory and His plans for you.*

BILLY GRAHAM

WHEN TIMES
ARE *REALLY* TOUGH

*God blesses the people who patiently endure
testing and temptation. Afterward they will
receive the crown of life that God
has promised to those who love him.*

JAMES 1:12 NLT

Tough times. Disappointments. Hardship. Pain. These experiences are the inevitable cost that each of us must pay for being human. When we're faced with these hardships, we may feel anxious or afraid. Thankfully, we must never encounter adversity alone. God is always with us.

When we are anxious or fearful, God stands ready and willing to protect us. Our responsibility, of course, is to ask Him for protection. When we call upon Him in prayer, He will answer—in His own time and in His own way.

If you find yourself enduring difficult circumstances, remember that God remains in His heaven. If you become discouraged with the direction of your day or your life, turn your thoughts and prayers to Him. He is a God of possibility, not negativity. He will guide you through your difficulties and beyond them. And then, with a renewed spirit of optimism and hope, you can thank the Giver for gifts that are simply too numerous to count.

MORE FROM GOD'S WORD

We are hard-pressed on every side,
yet not crushed; we are perplexed,
but not in despair.
2 CORINTHIANS 4:8 NKJV

He heals the brokenhearted
and binds up their wounds.
PSALM 147:3 HCSB

The LORD is my shepherd; I shall not want.
PSALM 23:1 KJV

The LORD is my rock, my fortress, and my deliverer,
my God, my mountain where I seek refuge.
My shield, the horn of my salvation, my stronghold,
my refuge, and my Savior.
2 SAMUEL 22:2-3 HCSB

I called to the LORD in my distress;
I called to my God. From His temple
He heard my voice.
2 SAMUEL 22:7 HCSB

MORE THOUGHTS
ABOUT TOUGH TIMES

We should not be upset when unexpected and upsetting things happen. God, in his wisdom, means to make something of us which we have not yet attained, and He is dealing with us accordingly.

J. I. PACKER

The only way to learn a strong faith is to endure great trials. I have learned my faith by standing firm amid the most severe of tests.

GEORGE MUELLER

Adversity is not simply a tool. It is God's most effective tool for the advancement of our spiritual lives. The circumstances and events that we see as setbacks are oftentimes the very things that launch us into periods of intense spiritual growth. Once we begin to understand this, and accept it as a spiritual fact of life, adversity becomes easier to bear.

CHARLES STANLEY

Our loving God uses difficulty in our lives to burn away the sin of self and build faith and spiritual power.

BILL BRIGHT

REMEMBER THIS

Today, remember that tough times are simply opportunities to trust God completely and to find strength in Him. And remember: Tough times can also be times of intense personal growth.

GET PRACTICAL

Talk about it . . . If you're having tough times, don't hit the panic button and don't keep everything bottled up inside. Talk things over with your spouse, and if necessary, find a counselor you can really trust. A second opinion (or, for that matter, a third, fourth, or fifth opinion) is usually helpful. So if your troubles seem overwhelming, be willing to seek outside help—starting, of course, with your pastor.

—m—

A CONVERSATION STARTER

Talk to a friend about ways that tough times can help you grow spiritually and emotionally.

NOTES TO YOURSELF

Write down your ideas about the best ways to find the courage and strength you'll need whenever you encounter tough times.

I need to remember to talk to god at all times. especially when times are tough. I tend to get very upset & I need to just stop & breathe & talk to god

3

THE QUESTION

How can the fear of God help me overcome
earthly fears?

THE ANSWER

When you have a healthy respect for God's
power—and when you fear displeasing Him—
you'll be able to keep earthly fears in perspective.

*The remarkable thing about fearing God is that
when you fear God, you fear nothing else, whereas
if you do not fear God, you fear everything else.*
OSWALD CHAMBERS

THE RIGHT KIND OF FEAR

*The fear of the L*ord *is the beginning of knowledge,
but fools despise wisdom and instruction.*

<small>Proverbs 1:7 NKJV</small>

Our unspoken fears have the power to hijack our thoughts and derail our emotions. These vague anxieties can cause us great harm. But there's a healthy kind of fear that we, as Christians, are instructed to embrace and cultivate. That fear, of course, is the fear of God.

Do you have a healthy, fearful respect for God's power? If so, you are both wise and obedient. And, because you are a thoughtful believer, you also understand that genuine wisdom begins with a profound appreciation for God's limitless power. When you have a healthy fear of your Creator, you can keep your concerns in proper perspective.

God praises humility and punishes pride. That's why God's greatest servants will always be those humble men and women who care less for their own glory and more for God's glory. In God's kingdom, the only way to achieve greatness is to shun it. And the only way to be wise is to understand these facts: God is great; He is all-knowing; and He is all-powerful. We must respect Him, and we must humbly obey His commandments, or we must accept the consequences of our misplaced pride.

MORE FROM GOD'S WORD

When all has been heard,
the conclusion of the matter is:
fear God and keep His commands.
ECCLESIASTES 12:13 HCSB

You shall walk after the Lord your God
and fear Him, and keep His commandments
and obey His voice; you shall serve Him
and hold fast to Him.
DEUTERONOMY 13:4 NKJV

The fear of the LORD is a fountain of life.
PROVERBS 14:27 NKJV

Respect for the LORD will teach you wisdom.
If you want to be honored, you must be humble.
PROVERBS 15:33 NCV

Honour all men. Love the brotherhood.
Fear God. Hounor the king.
1 PETER 2:17 KJV

MORE THOUGHTS ABOUT THE FEAR OF GOD

*When God is in sharp focus,
then life is also undistorted.*

ELIZABETH GEORGE

*Decisions become easier and simpler
where they are made not in the fear of men,
but only in the sight of God.*

DIETRICH BONHOEFFER

*Christ is either Lord of all,
or He is not Lord at all.*

HUDSON TAYLOR

*It is impossible to please God doing things
motivated by and produced by the flesh.*

BILL BRIGHT

*The greatest hindrance to Satan's destructive
efforts is our standing strong
in the knowledge and fear of the Lord.*

BILLY GRAHAM

REMEMBER THIS

The fear of God is the right kind of fear. Your respect for Him should make you fearful of disobeying Him . . . *very* fearful.

GET PRACTICAL

Obedience is a practical way to express your love and respect for God. Anne Graham Lotz correctly observed, "If you want to discover your spiritual gifts, start obeying God. As you serve Him, you will find that He has given you the gifts that are necessary to follow through in obedience."

—◊—

A CONVERSATION STARTER

Talk to a friend about what it means to fear God and why a healthy fear of the Lord is an important part of the Christian experience.

NOTES TO YOURSELF

Write down your thoughts about the importance of fearing God's displeasure and the dangers of putting the world's values ahead of His commandments.

I am extremely fearful that I disappoint god that I will not go to heaven. that he will take every thing & person from me & he will punish me severly

4

THE QUESTION

The Bible makes many promises.
But when anxieties and fears arise, I wonder:
Can I really depend upon those promises?

THE ANSWER

Yes! God is always faithful, and His Word
endures forever. So you should carve
out time every day to read the Word
and explore God's promises. When you do,
your fears will fade and your faith will grow.

*There are four words I wish we would never forget,
and they are, "God keeps his word."*

Charles Swindoll

WHEN YOU'RE AFRAID, YOU CAN TRUST GOD'S PROMISES

*The LORD is my light and my salvation—
whom should I fear? The LORD is the stronghold
of my life—of whom should I be afraid?*

PSALM 27:1 HCSB

When fears crop up—and they will—we Christians possess a source of strength that never fails. That source is God's Word. The Bible contains promises upon which we, as believers, can and must depend. But sometimes, especially when we find ourselves caught in the inevitable entanglements of life, we fail to trust God completely.

Are you tired? Discouraged? Fearful? Be comforted and trust the promises that God has made to you. Are you worried or anxious? Be confident in God's power. Do you see a difficult future ahead? Be courageous and call upon God. He will protect you and then use you according to His purposes. Are you confused? Listen to the quiet voice of your heavenly Father. He is not a God of confusion. Talk with Him; listen to Him; trust Him, and trust His promises. He is steadfast, and He is your Protector . . . forever.

MORE FROM GOD'S WORD

Let us hold on to the confession
of our hope without wavering,
for He who promised is faithful.
Hebrews 10:23 HCSB

As for God, his way is perfect:
the word of the Lord is tried:
he is a buckler to all those that trust in him.
Psalm 18:30 KJV

They will bind themselves to the Lord
with an eternal covenant that
will never again be forgotten.
Jeremiah 50:5 NLT

My God is my rock, in whom I take refuge,
my shield and the horn of my salvation.
2 Samuel 22:2-3 NIV

He heeded their prayer,
because they put their trust in him.
1 Chronicles 5:20 NKJV

MORE THOUGHTS ABOUT GOD'S PROMISES

Fear and doubt are conquered by a faith that rejoices. And faith can rejoice because the promises of God are as certain as God Himself.

KAY ARTHUR

God does not give us everything we want, but He does fulfill all His promises as He leads us along the best and straightest paths to Himself.

DIETRICH BONHOEFFER

The promises of Scripture are not mere pious hopes or sanctified guesses. They are more than sentimental words to be printed on decorated cards for Sunday School children. They are eternal verities. They are true. There is no perhaps about them.

PETER MARSHALL

It is an act of simplicity to choose to believe God, but it is also is an act of profound complexity as God literally moves in wondrous ways throughout the universe to keep His word.

BILL BRIGHT

REMEMBER THIS

God's Word never changes. The Lord will most certainly keep His promises to you. Your job is to keep your obligations to Him.

GET PRACTICAL

Never stop studying God's Word. Even if you've been studying the Bible for many years, you've still got lots to learn. Bible study should be a daily, lifelong endeavor; make it *your* daily, lifelong endeavor.

A CONVERSATION STARTER

Talk to a friend about the importance of Bible study and the need to use God's Word as a guidebook of how He keeps His promises in every situation.

NOTES TO YOURSELF

Write down your thoughts about God's promises and about the direction He is leading you today.

Sometimes I forget that no matter what we have or are going through God always gets us through it. His love & promise always comes through.

today - don't worry! his promise is he is here to help

5

THE QUESTION

When fear grips my heart, I seem to lose control of my thoughts. What should I do?

THE ANSWER

Sometimes, it takes effort to fill your mind with good thoughts. When you're gripped by anxiety or fear, you must be diligent in prayer, and be attentive to the things you're telling yourself. If your inner voice is predicting catastrophe at every turn, you should catch yourself before you talk yourself into a fear-induced panic attack.
And if your inner voice is, in reality, your inner critic, you must tone down the self-criticism. While you're at it, you can train yourself to recognize— and to reject—negative thoughts before they hijack your emotions and ruin your day.

Your thoughts are the determining factor as to whose mold you are conformed to. Control your thoughts and you control the direction of your life.

CHARLES STANLEY

CHANGING THE DIRECTION OF YOUR THOUGHTS

*Finally, brothers and sisters, whatever is true,
whatever is noble, whatever is right, whatever is
pure, whatever is lovely, whatever is admirable—
if anything is excellent or praiseworthy—
think about such things.*

Philippians 4:8 NIV

Because we are human, we are always busy with our thoughts. We simply can't help ourselves. Our brains never shut off, and even while we're sleeping, we mull things over in our minds. The question is not *if* we will think; the question is *how* we will think and *what* we will choose to think about. Our thoughts have the power to lift us up or drag us down; they have the power to energize us or deplete us, to inspire us to greater accomplishments, or to make those accomplishments impossible.

When you decided to allow Christ to rule over your heart, you entitled yourself to share in His promise of spiritual abundance and eternal joy. Have you claimed that entitlement? Are you a courageous believer, a person whose hopes and dreams are alive and well? Hopefully so. But sometimes, when pessimism and fear invade your thoughts, you may not feel like celebrating. If you've allowed anxiety to hijack your mind and heart, you must spend more time thinking positively about your blessings and less time focusing on your fears. Then, you should take time to thank the Creator for gifts that are, in truth, far too numerous to count.

Today and every day, think optimistically about your world and your life. It's the wise way to use your mind. And besides, since you will always be busy with your thoughts, you might as well make those thoughts pleasing (to God) and helpful (to you and yours).

MORE FROM GOD'S WORD

Set your mind on things above,
not on things on the earth.
COLOSSIANS 3:2 NKJV

The peace of God, which surpasses
all understanding, will guard your hearts
and minds through Christ Jesus.
PHILIPPIANS 4:7 NKJV

Guard your heart above all else,
for it is the source of life.
PROVERBS 4:23 HCSB

And do not be conformed to this world,
but be transformed by the renewing of your mind,
so that you may prove what the will of God is,
that which is good and acceptable and perfect.
ROMANS 12:2 NASB

For to be carnally minded is death,
but to be spiritually minded is life and peace.
ROMANS 8:6 NKJV

MORE THOUGHTS ABOUT CHANGING THE DIRECTION OF YOUR THOUGHTS

It is the thoughts and intents of the heart that shape a person's life.

JOHN ELDREDGE

We must have a decisive conviction that we are going to face trials with a joyful attitude. It is the joy of one who counts it a privilege to have his faith tested because he knows the testing will draw him closer to the Savior.

JOHN MACARTHUR

The things we think are the things that feed our souls. If we think on pure and lovely things, we shall grow pure and lovely like them; and the converse is equally true.

HANNAH WHITALL SMITH

Attitude is the mind's paintbrush; it can color any situation.

BARBARA JOHNSON

The mind is like a clock that is constantly running down. It has to be wound up daily with good thoughts.

FULTON J. SHEEN

REMEMBER THIS

When you experience tough times (and you will), a positive attitude makes a big difference in the way you tackle your problems. Your thoughts have the power to lift you up or bring you down, so you should guard your thoughts very carefully.

GET PRACTICAL

Watch what you think. If your inner voice is like a broken record that keeps repeating negative thoughts, you must guard your heart more carefully. And while you're at it, you should train yourself to begin thinking thoughts that are more rational, more positive, more forgiving, and less destructive.

—⁓—

A CONVERSATION STARTER

Talk to a friend about the fact that the quality of your thoughts affects the quality of your life.

NOTES TO YOURSELF

Write down a few practical things you can do to overcome anxiety, worry, fear, or procrastination.

_____

_____

_____

_____

_____

_____

_____

_____

_____

_____

_____

6

THE QUESTION

When times are good, it's easy to trust God. But, when tough times arrive, it's harder to trust Him. What does the Bible say about that?

THE ANSWER

The Bible makes it clear: God is always in control, and He loves us. So, when life seems unfair, we must try spending less time dwelling on "the unfairness of it all" and more time trusting Him. God's love is perfect, and perfect love casts out fear.

Contentment is trusting God even when things seem out of control.

CHARLES STANLEY

TRUST CASTS OUT FEAR

*Trust in the L*ORD *with all your heart, and lean
not on your own understanding; in all your ways
acknowledge Him, and He shall direct your paths.*
PROVERBS 3:5-6 NKJV

If we believe in God, we should trust Him. Yet sometimes, when we are besieged by fears and doubts, trusting God is hard indeed. Trusting God means entrusting Him with every aspect of our lives as we follow His commandments and pray for His guidance. When we experience the inevitable anxieties and pains of life here on earth, we must accept God's will and seek His healing touch. And at times, we must be willing to wait patiently for God to reveal plans that only He can see.

Trust has a way of casting out fear, and perfect trust—if we could manage to achieve it—would cast out fear perfectly. So the more we trust our heavenly Father, the sooner we can overcome our fears and discover the abundant life He has promised.

As you face the inevitable worries and hardships of everyday life, whom will you trust? Will you trust God completely and feed your mind with His promises? And will you trust His plans even when you don't understand them? Hopefully so, because His plans and His promises are waiting for you there, inside the covers of a book like no other: His book. It contains the essential wisdom you'll need to navigate the seas of life and land safely on that distant shore.

MORE FROM GOD'S WORD

In quietness and trust is your strength.
Isaiah 30:15 NASB

The Lord is my rock, my fortress,
and my deliverer, my God,
my mountain where I seek refuge.
My shield, the horn of my salvation,
my stronghold, my refuge, and my Savior.
2 Samuel 22:2-3 HCSB

The fear of man is a snare,
but the one who trusts in the Lord is protected.
Proverbs 29:25 HCSB

Those who trust in the Lord are like Mount Zion.
It cannot be shaken; it remains forever.
Psalm 125:1 HCSB

Jesus said, "Don't let your hearts be troubled.
Trust in God, and trust in me."
John 14:1 NCV

MORE THOUGHTS ABOUT TRUSTING GOD

In God's faithfulness lies eternal security.
CORRIE TEN BOOM

One of the marks of spiritual maturity is the quiet confidence that God is in control, without the need to understand why he does what he does.
CHARLES SWINDOLL

When a train goes through a tunnel and it gets dark, you don't throw away your ticket and jump off. You sit still and trust the engineer.
CORRIE TEN BOOM

When trust is perfect and there is no doubt, prayer is simply the outstretched hand ready to receive.
E. M. BOUNDS

Never yield to gloomy anticipation.
Place your hope and confidence in God.
He has no record of failure.
LETTIE COWMAN

REMEMBER THIS

The Lord loves you, and He wants to bless you abundantly and eternally. When you trust Him completely and obey Him faithfully, you will be blessed.

GET PRACTICAL

Because God is faithful, you can—and should—live courageously. When you feel anxious or afraid, trust God and do the courageous thing.

A CONVERSATION STARTER

Talk to a friend about what it means to really trust God. Why is trust important and how does trust dispel fear?

NOTES TO YOURSELF

Write down your own thoughts about the rewards of trusting God and the dangers of ignoring Him.

_____

_____

_____

_____

_____

_____

_____

_____

_____

_____

_____

_____

_____

7

THE QUESTION

When fears hijack my emotions, my thoughts seem to spiral out of control. What can I do to redirect my thoughts and calm my spirit?

THE ANSWER

One thing you can do to calm your fears is to pray early and often about the things that concern you. Prayer is a powerful tool you can use to redirect your day and your life. So pray early and often. The more you talk to God, the more He will comfort you.

Call upon God. Prayer itself can defuse fear.
BILL HYBELS

PRAYER CAN DEFEAT ANXIETY AND FEAR

Rejoice always, pray without ceasing,
in everything give thanks; for this is the will
of God in Christ Jesus for you.
1 Thessalonians 5:16-18 NKJV

The power of prayer": these words are so familiar, yet sometimes we forget what they mean. Prayer is a powerful tool for communicating with our Creator; it is an opportunity to commune with the Giver of all things good. Prayer is not a thing to be taken lightly or to be used infrequently. But sometimes, amid the inevitable anxieties of everyday life, we may lose sight of God's presence. Instead of turning to Him for guidance and for comfort, we depend instead upon our own resources. To do so is a profound mistake.

In his first letter to the Thessalonians, Paul wrote, "Rejoice evermore. Pray without ceasing. In every thing give thanks: for this is the will of God in Christ Jesus concerning you" (vv. 5:15–18 KJV). Paul's words apply to every Christian of every generation.

When we weave the habit of prayer into the very fabric of our days, we invite God to become a partner in every aspect of our lives. When we consult God on an hourly basis, we avail ourselves of His wisdom, His strength, and His love.

So today, instead of turning things over in your mind, turn them over to God in prayer. Instead of worrying about your next decision, trust God to help you make it. Instead of focusing on your fears, think about your Father's love. Pray constantly about things great and small. God is listening, and He wants to hear from you. Now.

MORE FROM GOD'S WORD

Ask, and it will be given to you; seek, and you will find; knock, and it will be opened to you. For every one who asks receives, and he who seeks finds, and to him who knocks it will be opened.

MATTHEW 7:7-8 NASB

I desire therefore that the men pray everywhere, lifting up holy hands, without wrath and doubting.

1 TIMOTHY 2:8 NKJV

Is anyone among you suffering? He should pray.

JAMES 5:13 HCSB

Confess your trespasses to one another, and pray for one another, that you may be healed. The effective, fervent prayer of a righteous man avails much.

JAMES 5:16 NKJV

And whenever you stand praying, if you have anything against anyone, forgive him, so that your Father in heaven will also forgive you your wrongdoing.

MARK 11:25 HCSB

MORE THOUGHTS
ABOUT PRAYER

*A man who is intimate with God
will never be intimidated by men.*

LEONARD RAVENHILL

*Prayer connects us with
God's limitless potential.*

HENRY BLACKABY

*The story of every great Christian achievement
is the history of answered prayer.*

E. M. BOUNDS

*When a man is at his wits' end,
it is not a cowardly thing to pray.*

OSWALD CHAMBERS

*We must focus on prayer as the main thrust
to accomplish God's will and purpose on earth.
The forces against us have never been greater,
and this is the only way we can release God's
power to become victorious.*

JOHN MAXWELL

REMEMBER THIS

There's no corner of your life that's too unimportant to pray about, so pray about *everything*. Prayer changes things and it changes you. So pray.

GET PRACTICAL

Today, ask yourself if your prayer life is all that it should be. If the answer is yes, keep up the good work. But if the answer is no, set aside a specific time each morning to talk to God. And then, when you've set aside a time for prayer, don't allow yourself to become sidetracked. Give God your full attention by putting prayer at the very top of your daily to-do list.

A CONVERSATION STARTER

Talk to a friend about your experiences concerning prayer: times when your prayer life was meaningful and times when you found it hard to pray. How did the quality and quantity of your prayers dispel irrational fears and unspoken anxieties?

NOTES TO YOURSELF

Make a list of the things you need to talk to God about. Then, schedule a regular time each day to talk about them.

8

THE QUESTION

Sometimes, when I'm discouraged or afraid,
I wonder if God really cares about
my problems. My faith seems to fade
and fears take over. What should I do?

THE ANSWER

Here are some specific things you can do to cast
out fear: 1. Read God's Word every day;
2. Stay actively involved in your local church;
3. Talk to trusted friends, mentors, family members,
and your pastor; 4. Pray about your situation every
day. The more you pray, and the more you study
God's Word, the more often you'll be reminded
that your heavenly Father is watching over
you today, tomorrow, and forever. You are
important to Him, and He has a plan for you.
Because He loves you, you can feel secure.

He goes before us, follows behind us,
and hems us safe inside the realm of His protection.

BETH MOORE

REMEMBER:
YOU'RE PROTECTED

Let us hold on to the confession of our hope
without wavering, for He who promised is faithful.

HEBREWS 10:23 HCSB

The Bible makes this promise: God will care for us and protect us. In the sixth chapter of Matthew, Jesus made this point clear when He said,

"Do not worry about your life, what you will eat or what you will drink; nor about your body, what you will put on. Is not life more than food and the body more than clothing? Look at the birds of the air, for they neither sow nor reap nor gather into barns; yet your heavenly Father feeds them. Are you not of more value than they? Which of you by worrying can add one cubit to his stature? . . . Therefore do not worry about tomorrow, for tomorrow will worry about its own things. Sufficient for the day is its own trouble" (vv. 25–27, 34 NKJV).

This beautiful passage reminds us that God still sits in His heaven, and we are His beloved children. Simply put, we are protected.

God has promised to protect us, and He intends to fulfill His promise. In a world filled with dangers and temptations, God is the ultimate armor. In a world filled with misleading messages, God's Word is the ultimate truth. In a world filled with more frustrations than we can count, God's Son offers the ultimate peace.

Will you accept God's peace and wear God's armor against the dangers of our world? Hopefully so, because when you do, you can live courageously, knowing that you possess the ultimate protection: God's unfailing love for you.

MORE FROM GOD'S WORD

*As for God, His way is perfect; the word of the Lord
is proven; He is a shield to all who trust in Him.*
Psalm 18:30 NKJV

*The Lord is my rock, my fortress, and my deliverer,
my God, my mountain where I seek refuge.
My shield, the horn of my salvation,
my stronghold, my refuge, and my Savior.*
2 Samuel 22:2-3 HCSB

*Those who trust in the Lord are like Mount Zion.
It cannot be shaken; it remains forever.*
Psalm 125:1 HCSB

*So we may boldly say: "The Lord is my helper;
I will not fear. What can man do to me?"*
Hebrews 13:6 NKJV

*The Lord is my shepherd, I shall not want.
He makes me lie down in green pastures;
He leads me beside quiet waters.
He restores my soul.*
Psalm 23:1-3 NASB

MORE THOUGHTS
ABOUT GOD'S PROTECTION

*God does not promise to keep us out of the storms
and floods, but He does promise to sustain us
in the storm, and then bring us out in due time
for His glory when the storm has done its work.*

WARREN WIERSBE

*Our future may look fearfully intimidating, yet
we can look up to the Engineer of the Universe,
confident that nothing escapes His attention
or slips out of the control of those strong hands.*

ELISABETH ELLIOT

*Adversity is always unexpected and unwelcomed.
It is an intruder and a thief, and yet in the hands
of God, adversity becomes the means through
which His supernatural power is demonstrated.*

CHARLES STANLEY

*A God wise enough to create me and the world
I live in is wise enough to watch out for me.*

PHILIP YANCEY

*Prayer is our pathway not only
to divine protection, but also to a personal,
intimate relationship with God.*

SHIRLEY DOBSON

REMEMBER THIS

Earthly security is an illusion. Your only real security comes from the loving heart of God. If you've given your heart to God's Son, you are protected, now and always.

GET PRACTICAL

If you'd like infinite protection, there's only one place you can receive it: from an infinite God. So remember: When you live in the center of God's will, you will also be living in the center of God's protection. Focus on obeying God's Word and following His Son. When you do, you have absolutely nothing to fear.

―――〰―――

A CONVERSATION STARTER

Talk to a friend about what it feels like to sense God's presence and to experience His protection in the midst of everyday life.

NOTES TO YOURSELF

Write down ways that God has protected you in the past and the ways He has promised to protect you in the future.

....

....

....

....

....

....

....

....

....

....

....

....

....

9

THE QUESTION

When I am anxious or fearful, I experience an array of negative emotions. What should I do?

THE ANSWER

Remember that God wants you to guard your heart from the fears and distractions that might cause you to stray from His path. When you encounter situations that make you afraid, turn your thoughts and prayers to your Creator.

The more wisdom enters our hearts, the more we will be able to trust our hearts in difficult situations.

JOHN ELDREDGE

WHEN YOU'RE AFRAID, GUARD YOUR HEART

*Guard your heart above all else,
for it is the source of life.*
PROVERBS 4:23 HCSB

Here in the twenty-first century, distractions, frustrations, disasters, and angry eruptions are woven into the fabric of everyday life. Traditional media is brimming with bad news and social media has dramatically increased our contact with troubled personalities and troubling circumstances. As believers, we must remain vigilant. Not only must we resist Satan when he confronts us, but we must also avoid the people and the places where Satan can most easily deceive or tempt us.

Do you seek God's peace and His blessings? Then guard your heart above all else. When you encounter a fear-provoking situation or a difficult situation, stand firm. When you're faced with a difficult choice or a powerful temptation, seek God's counsel and trust the counsel He gives. When you're uncertain of your next step, take a deep breath, calm yourself, and follow in the footsteps of God's only begotten Son. Invite God into your heart and live according to His commandments. When you do, you will be blessed today and tomorrow and forever.

MORE FROM GOD'S WORD

The peace of God, which surpasses all
understanding, will guard your hearts
and minds through Christ Jesus.

PHILIPPIANS 4:7 NKJV

The one who keeps God's commands live in him,
and he in them. And this is how we know that he
lives in us: We know it by the Spirit he gave us.

1 JOHN 3:24 NIV

Finally, brothers and sisters, whatever is true,
whatever is noble, whatever is right, whatever is
pure, whatever is lovely, whatever is admirable—
if anything is excellent or praiseworthy—
think about such things.

PHILIPPIANS 4:8 NIV

The pure in heart are blessed,
for they will see God.

MATTHEW 5:8 HCSB

Flee from youthful passions, and pursue
righteousness, faith, love, and peace, along with
those who call on the Lord from a pure heart.

2 TIMOTHY 2:22 HCSB

MORE THOUGHTS ABOUT GUARDING YOUR HEART

*Above all, we must be especially alert
against the beginnings of temptation,
for the enemy is more easily conquered
if he is refused admittance to the mind and is met
beyond the threshold when he knocks.*

THOMAS À KEMPIS

*If we guard some corner of darkness in ourselves,
we will soon be drawing someone else
into darkness, shutting them out from the light
in the face of Jesus Christ.*

ELISABETH ELLIOT

*Our fight is not against any physical enemy;
it is against organizations and powers that are
spiritual. We must struggle against sin all our lives,
but we are assured we will win.*

CORRIE TEN BOOM

*Our battles are first won or lost
in the secret places of our will in God's presence,
never in full view of the world.*

OSWALD CHAMBERS

REMEMBER THIS

When times are tough, you should guard your heart by turning it over to God.

GET PRACTICAL

Today and every day, it pays to study your Bible. God's Word can guide your steps and guard your heart. Let your Bible be your guide.

———m———

A CONVERSATION STARTER

Talk to a friend about the rewards of obedience and the blessings that God bestows upon those who follow in the footsteps of His Son.

NOTES TO YOURSELF

Write down some things you can do to guard your heart when confronting difficult situations or powerful temptations.

....

....

....

....

....

....

....

....

....

....

....

....

....

10

THE QUESTION

Sometimes, when I'm anxious or afraid,
I feel like my strength is almost gone.
What can I do about that?

THE ANSWER

When you need strength, you should turn your
concerns over to God. You should pray often;
you should ask for His guidance; and, you should
ask Him to help you establish your priorities.
Don't try to do everything or please everybody.
Simply do your best and leave the rest up to Him.

*We can be tired, weary and emotionally distraught,
but after spending time alone with God,
we find that He injects into our bodies energy,
power and strength.*

CHARLES STANLEY

A SOURCE OF STRENGTH

*He gives strength to the weary,
and to him who lacks might He increases power.*
Isaiah 40:29 NASB

Even the most inspired Christians can, from time to time, find themselves running on empty. The demands of daily life can drain us of our strength and rob us of the joy that is rightfully ours in Christ. When we find ourselves tired, discouraged, or worse, there is a source from which we can draw the power needed to recharge our spiritual batteries. That source is God.

God intends that His children lead joyous lives filled with abundance and peace. But sometimes, abundance and peace seem very far away. It is then that we must turn to God for renewal, and when we do, He will restore us *if* we allow Him to do so.

Today, like every other day, is literally brimming with possibilities. Whether we realize it or not, God is always working in us and through us; our job is to let Him do His work without undue interference. Yet we are imperfect beings who, because of our limited vision, often resist God's will. And oftentimes, because of our stubborn insistence on squeezing too many activities into a twenty-four-hour day, we allow ourselves to become exhausted, or frustrated, or both.

Are you tired or troubled? Turn your heart toward God in prayer. Are you weak or worried? Take the time—or, more accurately, make the time—to delve deeply into God's Holy Word. Are you simply overwhelmed by the demands of the day? Pray for the wisdom to simplify your life. Are you exhausted? Pray for the wisdom to rest a little more and worry a little less. When you do these things, you'll discover that the Creator of the universe stands always ready and always able to create a new sense of wonderment and joy in you.

MORE FROM GOD'S WORD

My grace is sufficient for you,
for my power is made perfect in weakness.
2 CORINTHIANS 12:9 NIV

The LORD is my strength and my song;
He has become my salvation.
EXODUS 15:2 HCSB

It is God who arms me with strength
and keeps my way secure.
PSALM 18:32 NIV

Have faith in the LORD your God,
and you will stand strong. Have faith
in his prophets, and you will succeed.
2 CHRONICLES 20:20 NCV

Be strong and courageous, and do the work.
Don't be afraid or discouraged,
for the LORD God, my God, is with you.
He won't leave you or forsake you.
1 CHRONICLES 28:20 HCSB

MORE THOUGHTS
ABOUT FINDING STRENGTH

*We can be tired, weary and emotionally
distraught, but after spending time alone
with God, we find that He injects into
our bodies energy, power and strength.*

CHARLES STANLEY

*The strength that we claim from God's Word does
not depend on circumstances. Circumstances will
be difficult, but our strength will be sufficient.*

CORRIE TEN BOOM

*Faith is a strong power, mastering
any difficulty in the strength of the Lord
who made heaven and earth.*

CORRIE TEN BOOM

*The truth is, God's strength is fully revealed
when our strength is depleted.*

LIZ CURTIS HIGGS

*The same God who empowered Samson,
Gideon, and Paul seeks to empower my life
and your life, because God hasn't changed.*

BILL HYBELS

REMEMBER THIS

When you are tired, fearful, or discouraged, God can restore your strength. Whatever your weaknesses, God is stronger. And His strength will help you measure up to His tasks.

GET PRACTICAL

If you're energy is low or your nerves are frazzled, perhaps you need to slow down and have a heart-to-heart talk with God. And while you're at it, remember that God is bigger than your problems—much bigger.

A CONVERSATION STARTER

Talk to a friend about things you can do to acquire strength for your journey and hope for the future

NOTES TO YOURSELF

Write down your own ideas about ideas about how you can live a joyous life because God is your strength.

11

THE QUESTION

When I'm afraid or anxious, it feels like my faith
is being tested. What should I do?

THE ANSWER

Faith is the opposite of fear. But if you're anxious,
it doesn't necessarily mean that your faith is
lacking; it means that your faith is being tested by
circumstances that may be out of your control.
If so, it's helpful to remind yourself that the Lord
is always in control, and that He has a perfect
plan for your life. Today, like every other day,
provides yet another opportunity to do your
best and leave the rest up to your Creator.

Meet your fears with faith.
MAX LUCADO

FAITH OVERCOMES FEAR

Don't be afraid, because I am your God. I will make you strong and will help you; I will support you with my right hand that saves you.

Isaiah 41:10 NCV

The Bible makes it clear: Faith is powerful. In fact, faith has the power to cast out fear. So when we are afraid, we must turn our thoughts and prayers toward God—His love, His protection, and His promises.

With faith, we can move mountains. With it, we can endure any hardship. With it, we can rise above the challenges of everyday life and live victoriously, whatever our circumstances.

Is your faith strong enough to move the mountains in your own life? If so, you've already tapped into a source of strength that never fails: God's strength. But if your spiritual batteries are in need of recharging, don't be discouraged. God's strength is always available to those who seek it.

The first element of a successful life is faith—faith in God, faith in His promises, and faith in His Son. When our faith in the Creator is strong, we can then have faith in ourselves, knowing that we are tools in the hands of a loving God who made mountains—and moves them—according to a perfect plan that only He can see.

MORE FROM GOD'S WORD

Don't be afraid. Only believe.
MARK 5:36 HCSB

Blessed are they that have not seen,
and yet have believed.
JOHN 20:29 KJV

All things are possible
for the one who believes.
MARK 9:23 NCV

And he said unto her, Daughter,
thy faith hath made thee whole;
go in peace, and be whole.
MARK 5:34 KJV

For truly I say to you, if you have faith
as a mustard seed, you shall say to this mountain,
"Move from here to there," and it shall move;
and nothing shall be impossible to you.
MATTHEW 17:20 NASB

MORE THOUGHTS ABOUT FAITH

*A perfect faith would lift us
absolutely above fear.*

GEORGE MACDONALD

*Faith is not merely holding on to God.
It is God holding on to you.*

CORRIE TEN BOOM

*Faith points us beyond our problems
to the hope we have in Christ.*

BILLY GRAHAM

*I have learned that faith means
trusting in advance what will
only make sense in reverse.*

PHILLIP YANCEY

*Your trials and difficulties
are a golden opportunity
to illustrate your faith in God.*

ELIZABETH GEORGE

REMEMBER THIS

The quality of your faith will help determine the quality of your day *and* the quality of your life. If your faith is strong enough, you and God—working together—can move mountains.

GET PRACTICAL

Faith should be practiced more than studied. Vance Havner said, "Nothing is more disastrous than to study faith, analyze faith, make noble resolves of faith, but never actually to make the leap of faith." How true!

A CONVERSATION STARTER

Talk to a friend about the role that faith plays in your life. And while you're at it, explore ways that faith can dispel fear.

NOTES TO YOURSELF

Make a list of the mountains you can move—or more precisely the mountains you *will* move—when you move beyond fear and focus, instead, on faith—faith in your Creator, faith in your future, and faith in yourself.

12

THE QUESTION

What does Jesus have to do with my anxieties,
my worries, and my unspoken fears?

THE ANSWER

God's Word promises that Jesus is the light of the
world. And, the Lord wants His Son to be the light
of your life, too. When you're afraid, remember
that your relationship with Jesus can be—
and should be—the cornerstone of your life.
Everything else, including every single one
of your earthly concerns, should be secondary.

When you can't see him, trust him.
Jesus is closer than you ever dreamed.
MAX LUCADO

YOU'RE ENCIRCLED–
AND PROTECTED–
BY CHRIST'S LOVE

As the Father loved Me,
I also have loved you; abide in My love.
JOHN 15:9 NKJV

The next time you feel anxious or afraid, take a few minutes to slow yourself down and focus, not on your troubles, but on your relationship with God's only begotten Son. Whether you're standing triumphant atop the highest mountain or slowly struggling through the darkest valley, Christ's love for you never changes. In fact, He loves you so much that He willingly sacrificed Himself on the cross so that you might live with Him throughout eternity.

None of the things we fear can ever separate us from Christ's love. Even when we falter, He loves us. When we fall prey to the world's temptations, He remains steadfast. In fact, no power on Earth can separate us from His love. When we acknowledge this fact, we can garner the strength to face our troubles head-on, knowing that earthly setbacks are temporary but God's love is not.

Jesus can transform us. When we open our hearts to Him and walk in His footsteps, our lives bear testimony to His mercy and to His grace. Yes, Christ's love changes everything. May we welcome Him into our hearts so that He can then change everything in us.

MORE FROM GOD'S WORD

*I am the good shepherd. The good shepherd
lays down his life for the sheep.*
JOHN 10:11 HCSB

*No one has greater love than this,
that someone would lay down
his life for his friends.*
JOHN 15:13 HCSB

*For Christ also suffered once for sins,
the just for the unjust, that He might
bring us to God, being put to death
in the flesh but made alive by the Spirit.*
1 PETER 3:18 NKJV

We love him, because he first loved us.
1 JOHN 4:19 KJV

*For God so loved the world, that he gave his only
begotten Son, that whosoever believeth in him
should not perish, but have everlasting life.*
JOHN 3:16 KJV

MORE THOUGHTS ABOUT CHRIST'S LOVE

*If you come to Christ, you will always
have the option of an ever-present friend.
You don't have to dial long-distance.
He'll be with you every step of the way.*

BILL HYBELS

*This hard place in which you perhaps find yourself
is the very place in which God is giving you
opportunity to look only to Him, to spend time in
prayer, and to learn long-suffering, gentleness,
meekness—in short, to learn the depths of the love
that Christ Himself has poured out on all of us.*

ELISABETH ELLIOT

*Jesus has been consistently affectionate
and true to us. He has shared his
great wealth with us. How can we doubt
the all-powerful, all-sufficient Lord?*

C. H. SPURGEON

*He loved us not because we're lovable,
but because He is love.*

C. S. LEWIS

REMEMBER THIS

A realization of God's love crushes fear. Jesus loves you. His love can—and should—be the cornerstone and the touchstone of your life.

GET PRACTICAL

Today and every day, give thanks for Christ's sacrifice. It is the ultimate expression of His love for you.

A CONVERSATION STARTER

Talk to a friend about Christ's love: what His sacrifice means to you and what it means to be a true disciple of Jesus.

NOTES TO YOURSELF

Write down your thoughts about Jesus: what He means to you, and how your life has been changed by Him.

....

....

....

....

....

....

....

....

....

....

....

....

13

THE QUESTION

Sometimes, when times are hard
and the headlines are disheartening,
it's hard for me to be optimistic.
What does the Bible say about optimism?

THE ANSWER

God's Word promises that if you've given your
heart to Jesus, your eternal future is secure.
So even when times are tough, you can be joyful,
hopeful, and optimistic. God created you
in His own image, and He wants you to experience
joy, contentment, peace, and abundance.
But, He will not force you to experience these
things; you must claim them for yourself. If you
want to defeat your anxieties and fears, you'll
need the right kind of attitude: the positive kind.

*If our hearts have been attuned
to God through an abiding faith in Christ,
the result will be joyous optimism.*

BILLY GRAHAM

THE POWER OF OPTIMISM

This hope we have as an anchor of the soul,
a hope both sure and steadfast.
HEBREWS 6:19 NASB

Are you a passionate Christian who expects God to do big things in your life and in the lives of those around you? If you're a thinking Christian, you have every reason to be confident about your future here on earth and your eternal future in heaven. As English clergyman William Ralph Inge observed, "No Christian should be a pessimist, for Christianity is a system of radical optimism." Inge's observation is true, of course, but sometimes, you may find yourself caught up in the inevitable complications of everyday living. When you find yourself fretting about the inevitable fears and frustrations of everyday life, it's time to slow down, collect yourself, refocus your thoughts, and count your blessings.

God has made promises to you, and He will most certainly keep every one of them. So, you have every reason to be an optimist and no legitimate reason to ever abandon hope.

Today, trust your hopes, not your fears. And while you're at it, take time to celebrate God's blessings. His gifts are too numerous to calculate and too glorious to imagine. But, it never hurts to try.

MORE FROM GOD'S WORD

*The L*ORD *is my light and my salvation—*
*whom should I fear? The L*ORD
is the stronghold of my life—
of whom should I be afraid?
PSALM 27:1 HCSB

Make me to hear joy and gladness.
PSALM 51:8 KJV

But if we look forward to something we don't have
yet, we must wait patiently and confidently.
ROMANS 8:25 NLT

"I say this because I know what I am
*planning for you," says the L*ORD*.*
"I have good plans for you, not plans to hurt you.
I will give you hope and a good future."
JEREMIAH 29:11 NCV

Let us hold on to the confession of our hope
without wavering, for He who promised is faithful.
HEBREWS 10:23 HCSB

MORE THOUGHTS ABOUT OPTIMISM

Developing a positive attitude means working continually to find what is uplifting and encouraging.

BARBARA JOHNSON

The Christian lifestyle is not one of legalistic dos and don'ts, but one that is positive, attractive, and joyful.

VONETTE BRIGHT

Christ can put a spring in your step and a thrill in your heart. Optimism and cheerfulness are products of knowing Christ.

BILLY GRAHAM

Keep your feet on the ground, but let your heart soar as high as it will. Refuse to be average or to surrender to the chill of your spiritual environment.

A. W. TOZER

If you can't tell whether your glass is half-empty or half-full, you don't need another glass; what you need is better eyesight . . . and a more thankful heart.

MARIE T. FREEMAN

REMEMBER THIS

As a follower of Christ, you should be optimistic about your future here on earth and your future in heaven. The Lord is good, His promises are eternal, and your eternal future is secure. So why not be an optimist?

GET PRACTICAL

Today and every day, try to be a realistic optimist. Your attitude toward the future will help create your future. So think realistically about yourself and your situation while making a conscious effort to focus on your hopes, not your fears.

A CONVERSATION STARTER

Talk to a friend about the potential rewards of optimism and the potential dangers of pessimism.

NOTES TO YOURSELF

Write down why you think it's important (and helpful) to be optimistic about your future and your life.

....

....

....

....

....

....

....

....

....

....

....

....

14

THE QUESTION

Even though I'm a Christian,
I sometimes feel imprisoned by
the concerns of everyday life. When that
happens, there's no peace in my heart.
What does the Bible teach us about peace?

THE ANSWER

There are two ways that the Lord speaks to
us personally: our intellect (the mind) and our
emotions (the heart). The peace of God will
guard both. The Bible promises that God's peace
surpasses human understanding. When you take
your concerns to Him in prayer, you'll find it easier
to accept His peace. The more you trust God—
and the sooner you learn to turn all your troubles
over to Him—the quicker you'll experience
the peace that only He can give.

*Peace does not mean to be in a place where
there is no noise, trouble, or hard work.
Peace means to be in the midst of all those
things and still be calm in your heart.*

CATHERINE MARSHALL

FINDING PEACE

Peace I leave with you, My peace I give to you;
not as the world gives do I give to you. Let not your
heart be troubled, neither let it be afraid.
JOHN 14:27 NKJV

Peace with God. Peace with self. Peace with others. Do you possess that kind of peace? Have you found the genuine peace that can be yours through Jesus Christ, or are you still rushing after the illusion of "peace and happiness" that the world promises but cannot deliver? The words of John 14:27 remind us that Jesus offers us peace, not as the world gives, but as He alone gives. Our challenge is to accept Christ's peace into our hearts and then, as best we can, to share His peace with our neighbors.

When we accept God's grace, we overcome the passing hardships of this world by relying upon His strength, His love, His peace, and His promise of eternal life.

The Scottish preacher George McDonald observed, "It has been well said that no man ever sank under the burden of the day. It is when tomorrow's burden is added to the burden of today that the weight is more than a man can bear. Never load yourselves so, my friends. If you find yourselves so loaded, at least remember this: it is your own doing, not God's. He begs you to leave the future to Him."

Today, as a gift to yourself, to your family, and to your friends, claim the inner peace that is your spiritual birthright—the peace of Jesus Christ. It is offered freely; it has been paid for in full; it is yours for the asking. So ask. And then share.

MORE FROM GOD'S WORD

He Himself is our peace.
EPHESIANS 2:14 NASB

The peace of God, which passeth
all understanding, shall keep your hearts
and minds through Christ Jesus.
PHILIPPIANS 4:7 KJV

But the fruit of the Spirit is love, joy, peace,
patience, kindness, goodness, faith, gentleness,
self-control. Against such things there is no law.
GALATIANS 5:22-23 HCSB

"I will give peace, real peace,
to those far and near,
and I will heal them," says the LORD.
ISAIAH 57:19 NCV

These things I have spoken to you,
that in Me you may have peace. In the world
you will have tribulation; but be of good cheer,
I have overcome the world.
JOHN 16:33 NKJV

MORE THOUGHTS ABOUT PEACE

In the secret of God's tabernacle, no enemy can find us, and no troubles can reach us. The pride of man and the strife of tongues find no entrance into the pavilion of God. The secret of his presence is a more secure refuge than a thousand Gibraltars. I do not mean that no trials come. They may come in abundance, but they cannot penetrate into the sanctuary of the soul, and we may dwell in perfect peace even in the midst of life's fiercest storms.

HANNAH WHITALL SMITH

Prayer guards hearts and minds and causes God to bring peace out of chaos.

BETH MOORE

Jesus gives us the ultimate rest, the confidence we need, to escape the frustration and chaos of the world around us.

BILLY GRAHAM

God has promised us abundance, peace, and eternal life. These treasures are ours for the asking; all we must do is claim them. One of the great mysteries of life is why on earth do so many of us wait so very long to claim them?

MARIE T. FREEMAN

REMEMBER THIS

God's peace is available to you this very moment if you place absolute trust in Him. The Lord is your shepherd. Trust Him today, and you will be blessed now and forever.

GET PRACTICAL

God's peace can be yours if you open up your heart and invite Him in. He can restore your soul if you let Him. The rest is up to you.

A CONVERSATION STARTER

God's Word promises that we can experience the peace that passes all understanding. Talk to a friend about ways that both of you can discover God's peace.

NOTES TO YOURSELF

Write down your thoughts about facing your fears and finding real peace.

15

THE QUESTION

My world is changing faster and faster. And change isn't easy for me. What should I do?

THE ANSWER

First, remember that God doesn't change (and neither do His promises). Then, try to embrace the changes that you believe will have a positive impact on your faith and your life. If a big change Is called for, don't be afraid. Sometimes, one big leap is better than a thousand baby steps.

But I'm convinced the best way to cope with change, ironically enough, is to get to know a God who doesn't change, One who provides an anchor in the swirling seas of change.

BILL HYBELS

WHAT DOESN'T CHANGE

I am the Lord, and I do not change.
MALACHI 3:6 NLT

Change can be a fearful thing to endure, yet endure it we must. Here in the twenty-first, change is simply a fact of life. The world keeps changing and so do we. The question, of course, is whether the adjustments we initiate turn out to be improvements or impediments. To find the answer to that question, we must first consult a source of wisdom that does not change. That source is God.

God's Word teaches us that the Lord is a constant, unchanging source of wisdom and strength. Because our Creator is trustworthy, we can be comforted by the knowledge that our covenant with the God is everlasting and non-negotiable. The Lord has promised to keep His word, and that's precisely what He will do.

So, the next time you face tough times or unwelcome changes, remember that one thing never changes: God's love for you. Then, perhaps, you'll worry less, do your best, and leave the rest up to Him.

MORE FROM GOD'S WORD

The wise see danger ahead and avoid it,
but fools keep going and get into trouble.
PROVERBS 22:3 NCV

But grow in the grace and knowledge
of our Lord and Savior Jesus Christ.
To Him be the glory both now and forever. Amen.
2 PETER 3:18 NKJV

When I was a child, I spoke like a child,
I thought like a child, I reasoned like a child.
When I became a man, I put aside childish things.
1 CORINTHIANS 13:11 HCSB

Then He who sat on the throne said,
"Behold, I make all things new."
REVELATION 21:5 NKJV

To every thing there is a season,
and a time to every purpose under the heaven.
ECCLESIASTES 3:1 KJV

MORE THOUGHTS
ABOUT CHANGE

Stress is the intangible partner of progress.

CHARLES STANLEY

*The secret of contentment in the midst of change
is found in having roots in the changeless Christ—
the same yesterday, today and forever.*

ED YOUNG

*Christians are supposed not merely to endure
change, nor even to profit by it, but to cause it.*

HARRY EMERSON FOSDICK

*In a world kept chaotic by change,
you will eventually discover, as I have, that this
is one of the most precious qualities
of the God we are looking for: He doesn't change.*

BILL HYBELS

*More often than not, when something looks like
it's the absolute end, it is really the beginning.*

CHARLES SWINDOLL

REMEMBER THIS

Change is inevitable; growth is not. God will come to your doorstep on countless occasions with opportunities to learn and to grow. And He will knock. Your challenge, of course, is to open the door.

GET PRACTICAL

Sometimes our losses mean that we must start over, from scratch. As believers we can find comfort in the knowledge that whatever change we are experiencing, whether on the mountaintops of life or in the deepest valleys of despair, God is there with us. As Christians who trust in a loving God, we are protected, even when we may feel very vulnerable. When we encounter the inevitable inevitable changes of life, we do so with the ultimate armor: God's promises. God's love will heal us if we invite Him into our hearts. And the time to invite Him is now.

A CONVERSATION STARTER

Talk to a friend about the changes that you're facing today. Explore ways that you've been successful in dealing with change. And while you're at it, explore ways that you can improve.

NOTES TO YOURSELF

Write down some of the major changes that you're facing right now. Then, jot down your ideas about the best way to address these changes.

....

....

....

....

....

....

....

....

....

....

16

THE QUESTION

When I'm anxious, I feel stuck. And when it's hard
(or uncomfortable) for me to do something,
I tend to procrastinate. What should I do?

THE ANSWER

The habit of procrastination is often rooted
in the fear of failure, the fear of discomfort,
or the fear of embarrassment. Your challenge
is to confront these fears and defeat them. So,
if unpleasant work needs to be done, do it sooner
rather than later. It's easy to put off unpleasant
tasks, but a far better strategy is this: Do the
unpleasant work first so you can enjoy the rest
of the day. The sooner you face your problems—
and the sooner you begin working to resolve
them—the better your life will be.

*We must not sit still and look for miracles; up and
doing, and the Lord will be with thee. Prayer and
pains, through faith in Christ Jesus, will do anything.*

GEORGE ELIOT

WORK, DON'T WORRY

*Be strong and courageous, and do the work. Don't
be afraid or discouraged, for the LORD God, my God,
is with you. He won't leave you or forsake you.*

1 CHRONICLES 28:20 HCSB

Sometimes, our fears result from procrastination. We have important work that should be done, but we hesitate. And the longer we delay, the more anxious we feel. The antidote to these sorts of fears is simple: we must face the work before us, and we must get busy.

When you know that something needs to be done, you have a choice to make: you can either do the work that needs to be done, or you can put it off until later. If you form the habit of facing your fears and tackling your problems in a timely manner, you'll feel better about yourself (and you'll earn bigger rewards from life). But if you fall prey to the trap of procrastination, you'll pay a heavy price for your shortsightedness.

The world often promises instant gratification: Get rich—today. Lose weight—this week. Have whatever you want—right now. Yet life's experiences and God's Word teach us that the best things in life require heaping helpings of both time and work.

It has been said, quite correctly, that there are no shortcuts to any place worth going. So it's important to remember that hard work is not simply a proven way to get ahead, it's also part of God's plan.

Today, do yourself this favor: Don't look for shortcuts (because there aren't any) and don't expect easy solutions to life's big challenges (because big rewards usually require lots of effort). You inhabit a world in which instant gratification is rare, but the rewards of hard work are not. Shape your expectations—and your work habits—accordingly.

MORE FROM GOD'S WORD

Whatever you do,
do it enthusiastically,
as something done for
the Lord and not for men.

COLOSSIANS 3:23 HCSB

But this I say: He who sows sparingly
will also reap sparingly, and he who sows
bountifully will also reap bountifully.

2 CORINTHIANS 9:6 NKJV

The plans of hard-working people
earn a profit, but those who act
too quickly become poor.

PROVERBS 21:5 NCV

I must work the works of Him
who sent Me while it is day;
the night is coming when no one can work.

JOHN 9:4 NKJV

You see that his faith and his actions
were working together, and his faith
was made complete by what he did.

JAMES 2:22 NIV

MORE THOUGHTS ABOUT WORK

If you want to reach your potential,
you need to add a strong work ethic to your talent.

JOHN MAXWELL

It may be that the day of judgment will dawn
tomorrow; in that case, we shall gladly stop working
for a better tomorrow. But not before.

DIETRICH BONHOEFFER

We must trust as if it all depended on God
and work as if it all depended on us.

C. H. SPURGEON

Thank God every morning when you get up
that you have something which must be done,
whether you like it or not. Work breeds a hundred
virtues that idleness never knows.

CHARLES KINGSLEY

I do not pray for a lighter load,
but for a stronger back.

PHILLIPS BROOKS

REMEMBER THIS

Work has a way of making fear fade away. When you find work that pleases God—and when you apply yourself conscientiously to the job at hand—you'll be rewarded.

GET PRACTICAL

Here's a time-tested formula for overcoming procrastination: Have faith in God and do the work. It has been said that there are no shortcuts to any place worth going. Hard work is not simply a proven way to get ahead, it's also part of God's plan for all His children (including you).

A CONVERSATION STARTER

Talk to a friend about the potential rewards of hard work and the ways that action, promptly taken, can dispel fear.

NOTES TO YOURSELF

Write down the most important things that have been bothering you lately. Then, write down specific things you can do to address those issues today, this week, and this month.

17

THE QUESTION

When tough times arrive,
I sometimes lose perspective.
When that happens, what should I do?

THE ANSWER

When we lose perspective,
God's Word teaches us to slow down,
to calm down, and to pray. When you ask God
to restore your perspective, He will do it.

Earthly fears are no fears at all.
Answer the big question of eternity,
and the little questions of life fall into perspective.
MAX LUCADO

MAINTAINING PERSPECTIVE

Joyful is the person who finds wisdom,
the one who gains understanding.
PROVERBS 3:13 NLT

For most of us, life is busy and complicated. And sometimes, we experience life-altering circumstances that leave us fearful or confused. Amid the rush and crush of the daily grind, it's easy to lose perspective—easy, but wrong. When our world seems to be spinning out of control, we can regain perspective by slowing ourselves down and then turning our thoughts and prayers toward God.

Do you carve out quiet moments each day to offer thanksgiving and praise to your Creator? You should. During these moments of stillness, you will often sense the love and wisdom of our Lord.

The familiar words of Psalm 46:10 remind us to "be still, and know that I am God" (NKJV). When we do so, we encounter the awesome presence of our loving heavenly Father, and we are blessed beyond words. But, when we ignore the presence of our Creator, we rob ourselves of His perspective, His peace, and His joy.

Today and every day, make time to be still before God. When you do, you can face the day's complications with the wisdom and power that only He can provide.

MORE FROM GOD'S WORD

If you teach the wise,
they will get knowledge.
PROVERBS 21:11 NCV

The one who acquires good sense
loves himself; one who safeguards
understanding finds success.
PROVERBS 19:8 HCSB

Since you have been raised to new life with Christ,
set your sights on the realities of heaven,
where Christ sits in the place
of honor at God's right hand.
COLOSSIANS 3:1 NLT

Teach me, LORD, the meaning of Your statutes,
and I will always keep them.
PSALM 119:33 HCSB

Trust in the LORD with all your heart
and lean not on your own understanding.
PROVERBS 3:5 NIV

MORE THOUGHTS ABOUT MAINTAINING PROPER PERSPECTIVE

Joy is the direct result of having God's perspective on our daily lives and the effect of loving our Lord enough to obey His commands and trust His promises.

BILL BRIGHT

Live near to God, and so all things will appear to you little in comparison with eternal realities.

ROBERT MURRAY MCCHEYNE

The proper perspective creates within us a spirit of reaching outside of ourselves with joy and enthusiasm.

LUCI SWINDOLL

When you and I hurt deeply, what we really need is not an explanation from God but a revelation of God. We need to see how great God is; we need to recover our lost perspective on life. Things get out of proportion when we are suffering, and it takes a vision of something bigger than ourselves to get life's dimensions adjusted again.

WARREN WIERSBE

REMEMBER THIS

When you focus on the world, you lose perspective. When you focus on God's promises, you gain clearer perspective. So don't become unduly upset over the minor inconveniences of life, and don't worry too much about today's setbacks—they're temporary.

GET PRACTICAL

Assiduously divide your areas of concern into two categories: those you can control and those you cannot. Resolve to work diligently on the former and let God handle the latter.

A CONVERSATION STARTER

Talk to a friend about times that you've lost perspective. And talk about specific things you can do to maintain proper perspective in the future.

NOTES TO YOURSELF

Write down a few examples of times when you've lost perspective. Then, make note of ways you can improve your responses in the future.

18

THE QUESTION

When I'm overcome by fears and worries, what should I do? And where should I turn?

THE ANSWER

Carefully divide your fears into two categories: the things you can control and the things you can't control. Once you've done so, spend your time working to resolve the things you can control, and entrust everything else to God.

The fierce grip of panic need not immobilize you. God knows no limitation when it comes to deliverance. Admit your fear, and commit it to Him. Dump the pressure on Him. He can handle it.

CHARLES SWINDOLL

BEYOND THE WORRIES
AND THE FEARS

Cast your burden on the LORD,
and He shall sustain you;
He shall never permit the righteous to be moved.
PSALM 55:22 NKJV

Because we are fallible human beings struggling through the inevitable challenges of life here on earth, we worry. Even though we, as Christians, have been promised the gift of eternal life—even though we, as Christians, are blessed by God's love and protection—we find ourselves fretting over the inevitable frustrations of everyday life.

Where is the best place to take your worries? Take them to God. Take your concerns to Him; take your fears to Him; take your doubts to Him; take your weaknesses to Him; take your sorrows to Him, and leave them all there. Seek protection from the Creator and build your spiritual house upon the Rock that cannot be moved. Remind yourself that God still sits in His heaven and you are His beloved child. Then, perhaps, you will worry less and trust Him a more. And that's as it should be because the Lord is trustworthy, and you are protected.

MORE FROM GOD'S WORD

Therefore do not worry about tomorrow,
for tomorrow will worry about its own things.
Sufficient for the day is its own trouble.

MATTHEW 6:34 NKJV

Peace I leave with you; My peace I give to you;
not as the world gives do I give to you. Do not let
your heart be troubled, nor let it be fearful.

JOHN 14:27 NASB

Do not be anxious about anything, but in
everything, by prayer and petition, with
thanksgiving, present your requests to God.

PHILIPPIANS 4:6 NIV

Cast all your anxiety on him
because he cares for you.

1 PETER 5:7 NIV

Let not your heart be troubled;
you believe in God, believe also in Me.

JOHN 14:1 NKJV

MORE THOUGHTS ABOUT WORRY

Tomorrow is busy worrying about itself;
don't get tangled up in its worry-webs.
SARAH YOUNG

Worry is the senseless process of cluttering
up tomorrow's opportunities
with leftover problems from today.
BARBARA JOHNSON

Worry is a cycle of inefficient thoughts
whirling around a center of fear.
CORRIE TEN BOOM

Pray, and let God worry.
MARTIN LUTHER

Do not worry about tomorrow.
This is not a suggestion, but a command.
SARAH YOUNG

REMEMBER THIS

You have worries, but God has solutions. Your challenge is to trust Him to solve the problems that you can't.

GET PRACTICAL

When you're anxious or afraid, remember that procrastination doesn't make things better. Instead of avoiding your problems, you should face them head on, which means working as if everything depended on you and praying as if everything depended on God.

—⚍—

A CONVERSATION STARTER

Talk to a friend about ways to trust God more and worry less.

NOTES TO YOURSELF

Make a list of things you still worry about, but cannot change. Then pray about your list.

19

THE QUESTION

When I worry, it seems like fear hijacks my emotions, and it's hard for me to feel— or to share—love. What can I do about that?

THE ANSWER

Remember that God is love, and He wants you to share His love, even when you're worried or afraid. So, instead of retreating into an emotional shell, reach out to family and friends. When you experience true friendship or genuine love, you'll feel more confident.

Love is the seed of all hope. It is the enticement to trust, to risk, to try, and to go on.

GLORIA GAITHER

REACHING OUT IN LOVE

And now abide faith, hope, love, these three;
but the greatest of these is love.
1 CORINTHIANS 13:13 NKJV

When times are tough, it pays to reach out to family and friends. Why? Because love has a way of casting out fear. When we experience compassion and encouragement from our loved ones, our hardships seem easier to bear. Our task, simply put, is to give love and to receive it.

God is love, and He intends that we share His love with the world. But He won't force us to be loving and kind. He places that responsibility squarely on our shoulders.

Love, like everything else in this world, begins and ends with God, but the middle part belongs to us. The Creator gives each of us the opportunity to be kind, courteous, and loving. He gives each of us the chance to obey the Golden Rule, or to make up our own rules as we go. If we obey God's rules, we're secure; but if we do otherwise, we suffer.

Christ's instructions are clear: "'Love the Lord your God with all your heart and with all your soul and with all your mind.' This is the first and greatest commandment. And the second is like it: 'Love your neighbor as yourself.' All the Law and the Prophets hang on these two commandments" (Matthew 22:37-40 NIV). May we follow His two greatest commandments today, tomorrow, and forever.

MORE FROM GOD'S WORD

A new commandment I give unto you,
That ye love one another; as I have loved you,
that ye also love one another.

JOHN 13:34 KJV

Love is patient, love is kind.
Love does not envy,
is not boastful, is not conceited.

1 CORINTHIANS 13:4 HCSB

Beloved, if God so loved us,
we ought also to love one another.

1 JOHN 4:11 KJV

Above all, love each other deeply,
because love covers a multitude of sins.

1 PETER 4:8 NIV

And we have known and believed the love
that God has for us. God is love, and he who
abides in love abides in God, and God in him.

1 JOHN 4:16 NKJV

MORE THOUGHTS ABOUT LOVE

Live your lives in love, the same sort of love which Christ gives us, and which He perfectly expressed when He gave Himself as a sacrifice to God.

CORRIE TEN BOOM

It is when we come to the Lord in our nothingness, our powerlessness and our helplessness that He then enables us to love in a way which, without Him, would be absolutely impossible.

ELISABETH ELLIOT

Line by line, moment by moment, special times are etched into our memories in the permanent ink of everlasting love in our relationships.

GLORIA GAITHER

Those who abandon ship the first time it enters a storm miss the calm beyond. And the rougher the storms weathered together, the deeper and stronger real love grows.

RUTH BELL GRAHAM

Carve your name on hearts, not on marble.

C. H. SPURGEON

REMEMBER THIS

God loves you, and He wants you to reflect His love to those around you. The key to successful Christian living lies in your submission to the Spirit of God. If you're a Christian, God has commanded you to love everybody, including the saints, the sinners, and everybody in between.

GET PRACTICAL

Be creative. There are many ways to say, "I love you." Find them. Use them. And keep using them.

A CONVERSATION STARTER

Talk to a friend about practical ways to share Christ's message and His love. And while you're at it, consider what Christ's love means to you.

NOTES TO YOURSELF

Write down some creative ways you can demonstrate your love for family and friends.

20

THE QUESTION

Sometimes life is difficult. When I'm anxious or fearful for myself or my family, what should I do?

THE ANSWER

Ask God for strength and wisdom. And above all, trust the Lord to solve problems that are simply too big for you to solve. When you turn everything over to God, you can live courageously.

Down through the centuries, in times of trouble and trial, God has brought courage to the hearts of those who love Him. The Bible is filled with assurances of God's help and comfort in every kind of trouble which might cause fears to arise in the human heart. You can look ahead with promise, hope, and joy.

BILLY GRAHAM

FINDING COURAGE

Behold, God is my salvation;
I will trust, and not be afraid.
ISAIAH 12:2 KJV

As believers in a risen Christ, we can, and should, live courageously. After all, Jesus promises us that He has overcome the world and that He has made a place for us in heaven. So we have nothing to fear in the long term because our Lord will care for us throughout eternity. But what about those short-term, everyday worries that keep us up at night? And what about the life-altering hardships that leave us wondering if we can ever recover? The answer, of course, is that because God cares for us in good times and hard times, we can turn our concerns over to Him in prayer, knowing that all things ultimately work for the good of those who love Him.

When you form a one-on-one relationship with your Creator, you can be comforted by the fact that wherever you find yourself, whether at the top of the mountain or the depths of the valley, God is there with you. And because your Creator cares for you and protects you, you can rise above your fears.

At this very moment the Lord is seeking to work in you and through you. He's asking you to live abundantly and courageously, and He's ready to help. So why not let Him do it, Starting now?

MORE FROM GOD'S WORD

Be strong and courageous,
and do the work. Do not be afraid
or discouraged, for the LORD God,
my God, is with you.
1 CHRONICLES 28:20 NIV

Be on guard. Stand firm in the faith.
Be courageous. Be strong.
1 CORINTHIANS 16:13 NLT

For God has not given us a spirit of fearfulness, but
one of power, love, and sound judgment.
2 TIMOTHY 1:7 HCSB

I can do all things through Him who strengthens me.
PHILIPPIANS 4:13 NASB

But He said to them, "It is I; do not be afraid."
JOHN 6:20 NKJV

MORE THOUGHTS ABOUT COURAGE

*Do not let Satan deceive you into
being afraid of God's plans for your life.*

R. A. TORREY

*Jesus Christ can make the weakest man into
a divine dreadnought, fearing nothing.*

OSWALD CHAMBERS

*Faith not only can help you through a crisis,
it can help you to approach life after
the hard times with a whole new perspective. It
can help you adopt an outlook of hope
and courage, through faith, to face reality.*

JOHN MAXWELL

*When once we are assured that God is good,
then there can be nothing left to fear.*

HANNAH WHITALL SMITH

*Talk courage. We walk in the wilderness today
and in the Promised Land tomorrow.*

D. L. MOODY

REMEMBER THIS

If you trust God completely and without reservation, you have every reason on earth—*and* in heaven—to live courageously. And that's precisely what you should do.

GET PRACTICAL

Is your courage being tested? Cling tightly to God's promises, and pray. God can give you the strength to meet any challenge and overcome any obstacle. With God as your partner, you have nothing to fear.

A CONVERSATION STARTER

Talk to a friend about any important tasks that you've been putting off. While you're at it, explore some of the reasons that you've been procrastinating.

NOTES TO YOURSELF

Make a list of fear-provoking circumstances that have, until now, held you back. Then, write down specific, measurable, date-stamped steps you can take to get yourself unstuck.